Where land meets sea

EXPLORING THE EAST COAST IN PICTURES

with
Colin Jarman, Garth Cooper, and Dick Holness
Aerial photos by Patrick Roach

IMRAY LAURIE NORIE & WILSON

Published by
Imray Laurie Norie & Wilson Ltd
Wych House St Ives
Cambridgeshire PE27 5BT England
☎ +44 (0)1480 462114
Fax +44 (0)1480 496109
Email ilnw@imray.com
www.imray.com
2008

1st edition 2008

© Colin Jarman, Garth Cooper and Dick Holness

 Colin Jarman, Garth Cooper and Dick Holness have asserted their right to be identified as the authors of this work in accordance with the Copyright, Designs and Patents Act 1988.

© Plan: Imray Laurie Norie & Wilson Ltd 2008

© Aerial photographs: Patrick Roach and Imray Laurie & Wilson Ltd 2008

© Photographs: Colin Jarman, Garth Cooper and Dick Holness
 except where credited otherwise

ISBN 978 184623 159 9

British Library Cataloguing in Publication Data.
A catalogue record for this book is available from the British Library.

Printed in Singapore by Star Standard Industries Ltd

INTRODUCTION

Join us on a trip along the East Coast of England, famous for its big skies, sea views, winding creeks, sand, shingle – and mud!

Our journey starts at Lowestoft, once a premier fishing port and now rapidly being redeveloped as a yachting centre. We end at the mouth of the English Channel with the historic port of Ramsgate.

In between lie some of the best sailing and boating waters in Britain. Here we find rivers and creeks populated by the ghosts of Roman, Saxon and Viking settlers, who began a history that over two thousand years has seen the development of fishing, merchant trading, boat and shipbuilding – even smuggling. The Royal Navy has stamped its signature on the area through its famous dockyards at Chatham and Harwich and its wartime activities at Harwich and Lowestoft.

It is a coastline that has been and still is being shaped by the power of the sea. The continual movement of sand, shingle and mud along the coast moulds each river estuary, laying down new mud flats criss-crossed with strange patterns, so clearly shown in some of the excellent aerial photographs by Patrick Roach.

Anyone who feels that strange compulsion to go down to the sea, will, we hope, enjoy this journey and appreciate the strange, delicate patterns of mud and water, sea and sky.

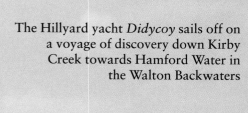

The Hillyard yacht *Didycoy* sails off on a voyage of discovery down Kirby Creek towards Hamford Water in the Walton Backwaters

Photo: Mike Perkins

The East Coast has a wealth of creeks and waterways both large and small, all waiting to be investigated. This expedition up the Blackwater and Chelmer Canal from Heybridge Basin to the shops at Maldon takes you through weedy waters overhung with weeping willows and new scenes, rural and urban, around every bend.

Lake Lothing lies between the commercial docks of Lowestoft and the Mutford Lock entrance to Oulton Broad. It is the home of several yacht harbours and boatyards, as well as the Excelsior Yard where the historic smack *Excelsior* (below), the last sailing trawler (now used as a training vessel for disadvantaged youngsters), is laid up each winter.

Once a bustling fishing port, Lowestoft is becoming a centre for East Coast leisure boating, as well as being the gateway from the North Sea to the fabled Norfolk Broads.

Southwold is synonymous with Adnams, brewers of fine East Suffolk ale. It also has an important lighthouse, unusually sited in the middle of the town, which uses red sector lights to keep mariners off shoals to the north and the Sizewell Bank to the south while giving guidance to the nearby harbour with its white light sector.

Southwold is also famous for its beach huts, which change hands for huge amounts of money. Attractions in the town include the cannon on Gun Hill and the Public Reading Rooms with their commanding views of Sole Bay, the venue for an important naval battle in 1672, which marked the beginning of the third Anglo-Dutch war.

Like a number of coastal towns and villages along this stretch of coast, the harbour at Southwold is some distance away from the town of the same name. In this case it's a mile south of the town on the estuary of the River Blyth. Surrounded by low lying marshland, each ebb tide carries hundreds of tons of silt from the upper reaches down the river and out to sea, as shown by the plume of brown stretching away from the entrance.

◄

Slaughden Quay, about half a mile south of Aldeburgh, right on the bend where the River Alde turns hard west, is where one finds the town's marine activity with sailing clubs, boat building and repair yards. Most of the beach fishing boats drawn up on the shingle along the town's seafront were built in the yards at Slaughden. So narrow is the neck of land at this point that a continuous programme of repair and replenishment is needed to stop the sea breaking through.

▶

The Snape Maltings concert hall is world famous. Once the centre of the Suffolk malting trade with barley shipped up the river Alde in Thames barges to the adjacent quay, it attracts thousands of visitors a year, some of whom still arrive by boat.

Shingle Street is aptly named, because the bank that keeps the sea away from this low-lying hamlet is entirely made of shingle, as is the bar at the mouth of the river Ore, which changes shape and position with successive North Sea gales. Once in living memory the bar completely closed the river entrance for several weeks. The River Ore runs parallel to the seashore inside Orford Ness, a giant shingle bank that stretches to Slaughden.

Orfordness Lighthouse (below) has been a beacon for sailors and fishermen for over 300 years. The present lighthouse is the third, each one having been built a little further eastwards as the Ness moved and changed.

Orford was a coastal port when the Normans landed on these shores. Its Norman Keep, all that remains of a major castle, dominates the low-lying countryside around. Today, Orford Quay is a centre for boating and the village boasts a fine smoked fish shop.

Considered by many to be the jewel of Suffolk, the River Deben discharges into the North Sea at Felixstowe Ferry, across a shingle bar rather like that on the Ore. Only nine miles long, the Deben boasts some of the most spectacular waterside scenery on the East Coast.

On the North bank, opposite Felixstowe Ferry is Bawdsey Manor, once the home of British radar research. Nearby stands the last of the old radar pylons, now a listed monument, which was erected before the last war and serves yachtsmen today as a prominent landmark.

Woodbridge is the quintessential East Coast town. Though nine miles from the sea, its influence on marine activity has been considerable. A key port in the wool and cereals trade from the region, a number of Nelson's ships of the line were built there and, more recently, many fine yachts. Opposite the town is the Sutton Hoo ship burial site that draws visitors from all over the world.

Inset: Boating is the key activity on Woodbridge's waterfront, which draws tourists and artists alike in their droves.

Sutton Hoo

Harwich Harbour has a history as long as men have taken to the sea. It's had close dealings with the Royal Navy, both through its victualling and building yards, and the HMS *Ganges* training centre on Shotley Point. It's long been a terminus for the ferries crossing to the near Continent and now has centres for both Trinity House and the shipping pilot service.

The Port of Felixstowe, on the northern shore,
is already one of the largest container facilities
in the world, yet it's set to nearly double its
capacity in the next five years or so.

The Orwell or Ipswich River was the lifeblood of Suffolk trade for centuries. This photo is of picturesque Pin Mill at low tide. About halfway up the river's navigable length, it was home to many Thames barges and even today it's possible to find two or three lying on the hard being worked on. The barge *Centaur* (left) evokes many memories as she sails serenely past Pin Mill village.

Few people get to see the true extent of the Ipswich Wet Dock, shown here with the New Cut (sweeping left), an extension of the river Gipping (from which Ipswich or Gyppeswyck gets its name). Once a thriving inland port, the Ipswich basin is being gentrified with luxury housing developments and is now a busy leisure boating centre. Commercial vessels no longer enter the old ship locks, but discharge and take on board cargo further down river at the Cliff Quay wharves.

The Walton Backwaters encompasses a large area of islands, saltings, marshes, meres and muddy creeks that are the haunt of birds, seals and wildfowl. It's a captivating place for naturalists and yachtsmen alike. It was made famous by Arthur Ransome in his book *Secret Water*, which was aimed at children but is still enjoyed by adults too. For many years the chart in the book was the most accurate available, because these waters are rarely surveyed by the Admiralty. The town of Walton on the Naze, whose outskirts are in the right hand corner of this picture, lies close to the head of Foundry Reach, the waterway in this photo, where the Walton & Frinton Yacht Club with its gated mooring basin, looks seaward down the creek. The town hard and the two boatyards can be seen on either side of the basin. At the right of the photo are the mudflats that used to be a public saltwater swimming area.

This extraordinary view of the Walton Backwaters shows the grandiose sweep of the Walton Channel from Stone Point (the sandy spit at top left) round to the Twizzle and Titchmarsh Marina, then on westward to Horsey Mere and the Wade. The inset photo shows the landmark Naze Tower, which stands close to the town of Walton on the Naze and is used for guidance by seamen from up and down the coast as well as inland in the creeks of the Walton Backwaters.

Brightlingsea, on the east bank of the River Colne, has a history going back to Roman times. Once a busy commercial port where many of the best Essex fishing smacks were built at the Aldous yard, it became a 'yachting' centre in the early 20th century. In the centre is Cindery Island. Most leisure craft moor in Cindery Creek (left side), leaving Brightlingsea Creek open for commercial traffic. The small creek at bottom left goes to St Osyth, another ancient town and priory. Opposite the entrance to Brightlingsea Creek, across the River Colne, is Mersea Island with the popular Pyefleet anchorage on its north (right hand) shore. This whole area is famous for its oysters.

West Mersea is one of the main boating centres on the East Coast. It stands at the entrance to the River Blackwater and has hundreds of yacht moorings filling its creeks. These carry names such as the Salcott Channel (on the left), then Thorn, Mersea and Besom Fleets – a 'fleet' being an area of shallow water. In the centre of the photo is a long, thin island called Packing Marsh Island, which gets its name from the oyster packing shed built in 1890 and still standing. The creek running round to the right along the Mersea town shore reaches the Strood (a raised roadway to the mainland). The enclosed water at the top of the photo is Aberton Reservoir.

From above, the Tollesbury saltings at low water show a wonderful, intricate pattern of runnels and gutways with just a few vein-like walkways and a scattering of boats in their mud berths. The retaining cill to the marina, keeping the water in at low tide, can clearly be seen at the head of Woodrolfe Creek. Beyond is the Tollesbury Cruising Club clubhouse and car park with the landmark block of white-fronted flats overlooking the open air swimming pool and the red roofs of the old fishermen's stores, built on legs to keep them above the tide.

The massive grey concrete blocks of the decommissioned Bradwell nuclear power station have been landmarks for sailors approaching the Blackwater for almost 50 years. Before that the tiny chapel of St Peter's on the wall, built in 654AD by St Cedd on the ruins of a Roman fort, was the main landmark for the area. Now trees mask it and it fades into insignificance beside the power station. Soon another landmark will appear with the construction of 10 large wind farm turbines and, possibly, a new nuclear power station alongside the existing buildings.

Osea Island in the middle of the upper Blackwater. This unusual view taken from the west end of the island and looking east along the length of the Blackwater towards Bradwell and Mersea, shows the causeway to the island and the shallows known as the Stumbles. The main river runs along the island's southern shore. There used to be a large heronry on the near (west) end of the island, but Dutch elm disease destroyed the trees and the herons moved away.

▼

▶

In the upper reaches of the Blackwater, opposite Northey Island (the site of the Battle of Maldon in 991AD), is the entrance to the 14-mile Blackwater and Chelmer Canal joining Heybridge to Chelmsford. In this photo the entrance lock at Heybridge Basin leads to the dark blue straight line of the canal, while to the left is a greenish flooded gravel pit and, further left, the winding Blackwater where it reaches the town of Maldon with its Hythe Quay, home to several Thames Barges.

Where now there are many moored boats in the Basin, years ago they were few and the left hand bank was lined instead with piles of seasoning timber.

Looking down the River Crouch from west to east. On the right is Wallasea Island and the Baltic Wharf where timber ships from the Baltic ports unload their cargoes. This timber is currently being used to construct the London Olympics facilities. Just down stream are the parallel pontoons of the Essex Marina. On the opposite shore is the Burnham Yacht Harbour, which was formed by digging a basin behind the seawall and then breaching the wall to allow it to flood. Despite the marina's capacity, there are still many yacht moorings off the Burnham waterfront. Opposite are the newly created Wallasea Wetlands and in the distance on the right is Foulness Island, home to a busy army firing range. The waterway to the right is the River Roach, which joins the Crouch downstream from the Wetlands.

The East Coast is littered with reminders of past conflicts; the early forts and earthwork ramparts thrown up to defend against the Vikings and Saxons and the Martello Towers of the Napoleonic wars. During the 1939-45 war a chain of forts carrying anti-aircraft guns was built across the mouth of the Thames to protect convoys and London itself. Several, such as these Red Sand Towers, still stand, despite being engineered to last only 10 years.

The longest pleasure pier in the world – Southend Pier pokes out 1.3 miles across the foreshore and mudflats, almost reaching the deep water channel of the River Thames where it enters the Estuary. The scale of the structure is apparent from the 80ft barge made tiny as she lies along the inland side of the pierhead.

Beside the Thames Barrier, officers of the Port of London Authority overlook the multiple gateways and control up to 4500 vessels passing through every month. Computer displays show what is happening everywhere on the tidal Thames and a duty officer of HM Coastguard sits at a nearby desk to co-ordinate rescues by London's lifeboats, which happen, on average, more than 650 times each year.

A ship bringing new cars to Britain fusses her way past buoys marking the wreck of the *Richard Montgomery*, heading for Sheerness and the mouth of the River Medway. The scene is idyllic, but beneath the glittering water in the holds of the *Montgomery* lurks enough WWII munitions to flatten everything for miles around.

Ancient names describe ancient places in this shimmering scene centred on Stangate Creek, off the River Medway. Sharfleet, Slayhills Marshes, Slaughterhouse Point, Bedlams Bottom, Burntwick Island – names going back centuries to times when the low-lying marshes were used as burial grounds, where the Plague dead were burnt and buried and before prisoners of war were locked up in old hulks at anchor in these lonely shallow waters.

For over 400 years, the Royal Dockyard at Chatham was a vital resource that kept the ships of the Royal Navy up to scratch. Ships left here to fight the Spanish Armada; the Dutch Admiral de Ruyter led a daring and successful raid on the fleet in the river and dockyard in 1667, sinking 16 ships; HMS *Victory* was built here and launched in 1765; and the last ship built here for the Royal Navy, the submarine HMS *Ocelot*, returned at the end of her active service and is on permanent display. The Navy has now left for good and commerce and leisure are steadily taking over what they left behind.

In the far distance, Chatham Maritime Marina now occupies No.1 Basin, while Nos.2 and 3 are still used occasionally by merchant ships.

In the top left of the photo three long grey shipbuilding sheds and slipways can just be seen, one of which now houses the National Collection of RNLI lifeboats. Hundreds of yachts are moored in the sweep of the River Medway with many more in the modern Gillingham Marina in the foreground.

The Swale snakes its way from the Medway, past acres of new cars, then the little town of Queenborough and its lines of moorings, thence beneath two bridges before heading off eastwards to cut Sheppey off from mainland Kent.

The smaller bridge carries trains across the Swale between Sheppey and the mainland and has to lift on request to let yachts and ships bound for Ridham Dock pass through. All road traffic on and off the island had to use this bridge too, until the new high-level road crossing opened. Where the Swale heads east from the left of the picture, another crossing can be made out – an ancient causeway at Elmley Ferry, the original main route across the waterway.

Low tide in the Swale outside Conyer Creek displays the intricate network of gullies and swatchways that are normally hidden beneath the water. In the middle distance, the light coloured patchwork of fields shows the extent of land reclamation – once this was all saltmarsh, flooded on the tide twice every day.

The fashionable town of Whitstable
basks in the afternoon sun, its tiny
harbour a lasting reminder of times past
when townsfolk depended upon the sea
and particularly oysters, for its
livelihood. On the left, the strange
shingle bank known as 'The Street'
extends far out to sea.

Herne Bay is a new town compared to its neighbour, Whitstable. There was little development here before the 19th century. Even the harbour is modern – the arm defends the seafront and was added in a piece of inspired planning. Beside it stands the inshore stump of what was once the second longest pier in the country.

East of Herne Bay, the ruin of the ancient church at Reculver broods over the estuary and Kentish flats wind farm. Still standing are some of the massive walls of the Roman fort of Regulbium and here, perhaps, lies King Ethelbert of Kent, who was baptised by St Augustine in 597AD and reputedly moved his royal court here. What is more certain is that in 669AD Ethelbert's great grandson, King Egbert, gave the land to a priest, Bassa, who initiated the building of a monastery, using the materials from the Roman fort.

The church began life as the minster for the monastery and was developed over the years, the twin towers being added in the 12th century. In 1809 local people feared the structure would be lost to coastal erosion and pulled much of it down to use for a new church on higher ground a mile away. Other parts of the structure became foundations for the pier at Margate. In 1910, Trinity House stepped in to safeguard the towers, recognising them for their value as a landmark for seafarers and securing the low headland on which they stand, sadly proving that the church could have been left intact after all. Today, the long term security of the towers is again in doubt as debate rages about the cost and practicality of defending our shorelines against rising sea levels.

The sandy beach and little harbour at Margate give way to low chalk cliffs running round to the North Foreland where the white lighthouse is just visible. By the sea-bathing pool set in the beach, a bronze lifeboatman stares out to sea, perhaps looking for his nine comrades lost when their surfboat capsized in 1897.

There has been a light on the North Foreland since 1499, overlooking the meeting of busy shipping lanes from the Thames, the North Sea and the English Channel. Some 500 years later, in 1998, the present lighthouse became the last in Britain to be automated.

Broadstairs was once a centre for ship building and smuggling, but now many follow in the footsteps of Charles Dickens and make it their favourite holiday resort.

This view of Ramsgate clearly shows the original 'Royal' Harbour, which now shelters a myriad of fishing boats and yachts, lying within the much larger port that was created when Ramsgate became a busy terminal for cross-Channel ferries. Originally, Ramsgate was a small fishing village with a wooden pier. However, the Great Storm of 1748, which decimated shipping anchored in The Downs off Deal, showed the need for a safe haven nearby and a new harbour was begun at Ramsgate shortly afterwards, its great stone piers largely built by prisoners of war. In 1820, King George IV embarked with the Royal Squadron at Ramsgate on his way to Hanover. In appreciation of the hospitality he received, he decreed that Ramsgate Harbour should have the right to add 'Royal' to its name. This status of Royal Harbour is unique in mainland Britain.

The harbour's early years were plagued by silting and the engineer John Smeaton remedied it by means of an inner basin (clearly seen in the photo) with sluices through its cross-wall, which would be opened at low water to drive the silt out through the entrance. Modern use of the harbour means that this can no longer be done and instead the harbour has to be dredged regularly – evidence of silting can be seen inside the old eastern pierhead.

A potent symbol of man's ingenuity and concerns about global warming, everything about these wind turbines is massive. Here on the Kentish Flats, in shallow waters five miles north of Herne Bay, 30 towers each rise 70m above sea level. Each rotor is 90m in diameter with the tips 115m above the sea at their highest point. (For comparison, Nelson's Column in Trafalgar Square is 52m high.) The whole installation can supply the electricity for 100,000 homes – when the wind blows. In practice, the average power developed is less than a third of the theoretical maximum and, of course, no power at all is forthcoming if there is not enough (or indeed if there is too much) wind. These strangely beautiful structures have to be matched by other, more constant power sources and will have to be removed at the end of their 20-year lifespan.

Lying peacefully at anchor,
bathed in evening sunlight, close
to where land meet sea.